Thumb Position for Beginners
Easy pieces for cello duet and cello/piano

Leichte Stücke für Celloduet und Cello/Klavier

Pièces faciles pour deux violoncelles et violoncelle et piano

Pat Legg & Alan Gout

© 1997 by Faber Music Ltd
First published in 1997 by Faber Music Ltd
Bloomsbury House
74–77 Great Russell Street
London WC1B 3DA
Music set by Jackie Leigh
Cover design by S & M Tucker
Printed in England by Caligraving Ltd
ISBN10: 0-571-51801-X
EAN13: 978-0-571-51801-2

To buy Faber Music publications or to find out about the full range of titles available
please contact your local music retailer or Faber Music sales enquiries:

Faber Music Limited, Burnt Mill, Elizabeth Way, Harlow, CM20 2HX England
Tel: +44 (0)1279 82 89 82   Fax: +44 (0)1279 82 89 83
sales@fabermusic.com   fabermusicstore.com

Contents / Table / Inhalt

1. French folk-song

2. Hopak

Notes used: A string ○ 1 2 3
D string ○ 1 2 3

Russian folk-song
arr. Pat Legg

3. Mattachins

Notes used: A string ○ 1
D string ○ 1 2 3

French dance

4. Belli bella bimba

© 1997 by Faber Music Ltd.

5. O waly waly

© 1997 by Faber Music Ltd.

6. Lovely Joan

Notes used: A string   ♀ 1 2 3
              D string   ♀ 1 2 3
              G string   3

English folk-song
arr. Pat Legg

7. Shalom chaverin

Notes used: A string ♀ 2 3
              D string ♀ 1 2 3
              G string   1

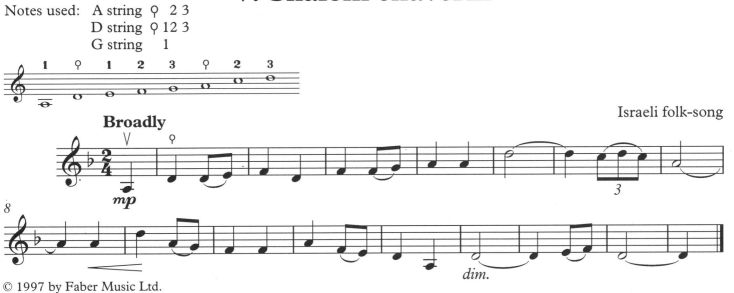

Israeli folk-song

Broadly

mp

3

dim.

8. Come all ye fair and tender maidens

Notes used: A string ♀ 1 3
              D string ♀ 1 3

English folk-song
arr. Pat Legg

Leisurely

Pupil

mf (2.*f*)

Teacher

mf (2.*f*)

dim.

dim.

9. Sleigh ride

Notes used: A string ♀1 2 3
             D string ♀ 12 3

Russian folk-song
arr. Pat Legg

* 2nd time, optional top D

10. Korean folk-song

Notes used: A string ♩ 2 3
D string ♩ 1 2 3
G string 3

Korean traditional
arr. Pat Legg

10

11. French carol

Notes used: A string ♁1
            D string ♁12 3
            G string   1

French traditional
arr. Pat Legg

Not too fast, with a slightly etherial sound

10. Korean folk-song

Notes used: A string ♢ 2 3
D string ♢ 12 3
G string 3

Korean traditional
arr. Pat Legg

11. French carol

Notes used: A string ♀ 1
D string ♀ 12 3
G string 1

French traditional
arr. Pat Legg

Not too fast, with a slightly etherial sound

12. Hunters' song

Notes used: A string   1 2
D string ♀ 1 2 3
G string ♀   3

Allegro vigoroso

English round

13. Summer is a coming in

Notes used: A string ♀ 1 23
                       D string ♀ 1 23
                       G string   3

English folk-song
arr. Alan Gout

14. Henry Martin

Notes used: A string ♀11223 4
D string ♀ 12 3
G string   3

British sea shanty
arr. Pat Legg

Lilting, like a boat

Pupil

Teacher

© 1997 by Faber Music Ltd.

Thumb Position for Beginners
Easy pieces for cello duet and cello/piano

Leichte Stücke für Celloduet und Cello/Klavier

Pièces faciles pour deux violoncelles et violoncelle et piano

Pat Legg & Alan Gout

PIANO PART

© 1997 by Faber Music Ltd
First published in 1997 by Faber Music Ltd
Bloomsbury House
74–77 Great Russell Street
London WC1B 3DA
Music set by Jackie Leigh
Cover design by S & M Tucker
Printed in England by Caligraving Ltd

ISBN10: 0-571-51801-X
EAN13: 978-0-571-51801-2

To buy Faber Music publications or to find out about the full range of titles available
please contact your local music retailer or Faber Music sales enquiries:

Faber Music Limited, Burnt Mill, Elizabeth Way, Harlow, CM20 2HX England
Tel: +44 (0)1279 82 89 82   Fax: +44 (0)1279 82 89 83
sales@fabermusic.com   fabermusicstore.com

CELLO TEACHING MATERIAL
FROM FABER MUSIC

PAT LEGG
Superstudies

*Really easy original studies for
the young player*

BOOK 1 ISBN 0-571-51378-6
BOOK 2 ISBN 0-571-51445-6

PAT LEGG and ALAN GOUT
Learning the Tenor Clef

*Progressive Studies and Pieces
for Cellists*

ISBN 0-571-51917-2

MARY COHEN
Superduets

*Fantastic cello duets
for beginners*

BOOK 1 ISBN 0-571-51891-5
BOOK 2 ISBN 0-571-51892-3

PAT LEGG and ALAN GOUT
Thumb Position for Beginners

*Easy pieces for cello duet
and cello/piano*

ISBN 0-571-51801-X

MARY COHEN
Technique takes off!

*14 intermediate studies
for solo cello*

ISBN 0-571-51420-0

PAT LEGG and ALAN GOUT
Thumb Position Repertoire

*Intermediate pieces
for cello and piano*

ISBN 0-571-51802-8

POLLY WATERFIELD
and GILLIAN LUBACH
Polytekniks

*Cello duets for musical and
technical accomplishment*

EASY ISBN 0-571-51490-1
INTERMEDIATE ISBN 0-571-51499-5

PAT LEGG
Position Jazz

*Up-beat, original pieces
for cello duet*

ISBN 0-571-51144-9

FABER ff MUSIC

Contents/Table/Inhalt

1. French folk-song – cello duet
2. Hopak – cello duet

3. Mattachins

French dance

© 1997 by Faber Music Ltd.

4. Belli bella bimba

Italian song

5. O waly waly

English folk-song
(Somerset)

6. Lovely Joan – cello duet

7. Shalom chaverin

Israeli folk-song

8. Come all ye fair and tender maidens – cello duet

9. Sleigh ride – cello duet

10. Korean folk-song – cello duet

11. French carol – cello duet

8

12. Hunters' song

Allegro vigoroso

English round

13. Summer is a coming in – cello duet

14. Henry Martin – cello duet

15. The coasts of high Barbary

English sea shanty

16. The great speckled bird – cello duet

17. Fukien boat song – cello duet

18. Hoi Hoi seal song – cello duet

19. The Grenadier and the Lady – cello duet

20. Out in the meadows

Israeli song

21. Ding dong bell

Old English song

22. Blow the wind southerly

English folk-song
(Northumberland)

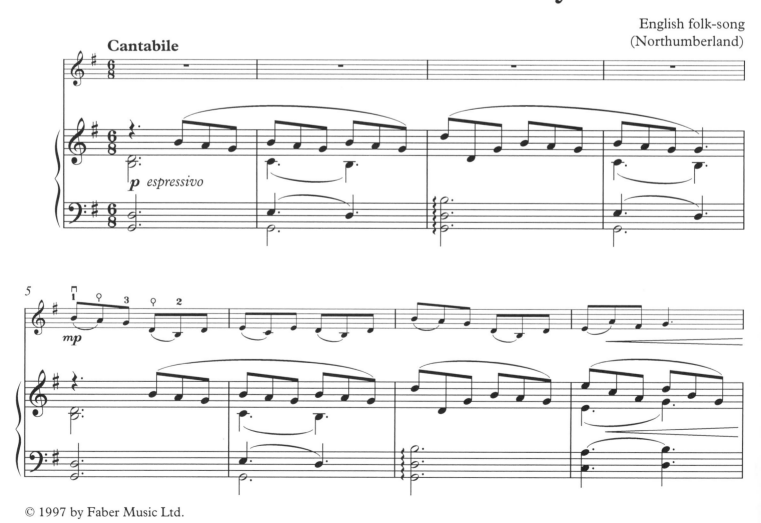

23. Alas! because of Adam's sin

French carol
(Breton)

* Make the melody sing.

24. School bells – cello duet

25. Buy my blooming lavender

Allegretto

English town-cry

26. Every night – cello duet

27. The Isle of Stronsay – cello duet

15. The coasts of high Barbary

Notes used: A string ♁ 1
D string ♁ 1 23
G string   2

English sea shanty

16. The great speckled bird

Notes used: A string ♁ 1
D string ♁ 1 23
G string   23

American
(Hillbilly gospel song)
arr. Pat Legg

17. Fukien boat song

18. Hoi Hoi seal song

Notes used: D string ♩ 1 2 3
G string ♩ 1 3

Scottish folk-song
arr. Pat Legg

19. The Grenadier and the Lady

Notes used: A string ♀1 2 3
D string ♀ 2 3

English folk-song
arr. Pat Legg

20. Out in the meadows

21. Ding dong bell

Notes used: A string ♀ 1 23 4
D string ♀ 1 2 3
G string 1

Old English song

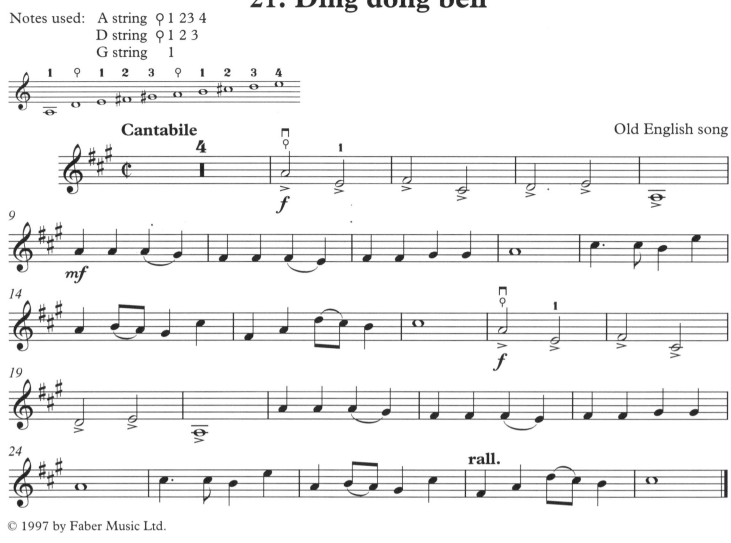

22. Blow the wind southerly

Notes used: A string ♀ 1 223 4
D string ♀ 1 23
G string 23

English folk-song
(Northumberland)

23. Alas! because of Adam's sin

Notes used: A string ♀1
D string ♀ 12 3
G string 1 23

French carol
(Breton)

24. School bells

Notes used: A string ♩ 1
                D string ♩ 1 2

Korean traditional
arr. Pat Legg

25. Buy my blooming lavender

Notes used: A string ♀12 3
D string ♀ 23

English town-cry

© 1997 by Faber Music Ltd.

26

26. Every night

Notes used: A string ○ 1 2 3
              D string ○ 1 2

American folk-song
arr. Pat Legg

27. The Isle of Stronsay